T0147095

LIGHT THE FIRE AGAIN

*Eighteenth-Century Light
for the Twenty-First-Century Darkness*

JAMES P. WILLIAMS

WESTBOW
PRESS®
A DIVISION OF THOMAS NELSON
& ZONDERVAN

This book is a work of non-fiction. Unless otherwise noted, the author and the publisher make no explicit guarantees as to the accuracy of the information contained in this book and in some cases, names of people and places have been altered to protect their privacy.

WestBow Press books may be ordered through booksellers or by contacting:

WestBow Press
A Division of Thomas Nelson & Zondervan
1663 Liberty Drive
Bloomington, IN 47403
www.westbowpress.com
844-714-3454

Because of the dynamic nature of the Internet, any web addresses or links contained in this book may have changed since publication and may no longer be valid. The views expressed in this work are solely those of the author and do not necessarily reflect the views of the publisher, and the publisher hereby disclaims any responsibility for them.

Any people depicted in stock imagery provided by Getty Images are models, and such images are being used for illustrative purposes only. Certain stock imagery © Getty Images.

Scripture taken from The Message. Copyright © 1993, 1994, 1995, 1996, 2000, 2001, 2002. Used by permission of NavPress Publishing Group.

Scripture taken from the King James Version of the Bible.

Scripture quotations taken from the (NASB®) New American Standard Bible®, Copyright © 1960, 1971, 1977, 1995, 2020 by The Lockman Foundation. Used by permission. All rights reserved. www.lockman.org

ISBN: 978-1-6642-4661-4 (sc)
ISBN: 978-1-6642-4660-7 (hc)
ISBN: 978-1-6642-4662-1 (e)

Library of Congress Control Number: 2021920592

Print information available on the last page.

WestBow Press rev. date: 12/16/2021

The wonderful discovery of a long-lost letter unfolding the narrative of William Robinson, Evangelist, and how God used him during the Great Awakening (1709–1746)

"Dedicated to Jesus, the Light of the World,
and Sally, my beloved wife.

A special thanks to Dr. Stephen Crocco, librarian,
Princeton Theological Seminary, and to our dear
Fellows in England, where the First Great Awakening
took place and spread to America's colonies.

At that moment, open-eyed, wide-eyed, they
recognized HIM. And HE disappeared. Back and
forth they talked, "Didn't we feel on fire as HE
conversed? HE opened up the Scriptures to us."
—Luke 24:31–32 The Message

Light the Fire Again is in the twenty-first century, and Satan
does not want you to find its potential firepower and be
blessed. Never before has this additional Great Awakening
power of Christianity truly been reached by following the
eighteenth-century light for the twenty-first-century darkness!

CONTENTS

THESIS

Thesis

"The Great Awakening, by all accounts, rocked in the 30's and 40's of the 18th century with a Spiritual Awakening that shook and stirred all aspects of the amorphous Christian settlements. There was more evidence than that in the New England Colonies (Massachusetts Bay; Rhode Island/Providence; Connecticut) and the Middle Colonies. (New York; New Jersey; Pennsylvania; Delaware) and the Southern Colonies (Maryland; Virginia; North Carolina; and maybe Georgia) where Robinson was an itinerant."[1]

Cit

William Robinson was, to the best of our knowledge, an itinerant evangelist in New York, New Jersey, Pennsylvania, Delaware, Maryland, Virginia, North Carolina—seven of the colonies, and perhaps eight with Georgia.

---

[1] Jeffrey, David Lyle, ed., *A Burning and a Shining Light: English Spirituality in the Age of Wesley* (Grand Rapids, MI: William B. Eerdmans, 1987), 40.

General Objectives

Knowledge, inspiration, and enlightenment of Jesus's servant William Robinson.

Specific Objectives

At the end of the book, readers will have encouragement to "Light the fire again" in their faith and ministries.

Six Cognitive Domains

1. Learn about Log College's contribution to the Great Awakening and Princeton University.
2. New, firsthand information on the Great Awakening from an autobiographical letter of William Robinson, and unconnected extant historical biography.
3. Examine some of the dependent variables of the Great Awakening touched on by William Robinson's letter (excerpts).
4. Learn through peers how William Robinson was perceived as a yokefellow via:
   1. George Whitfield
   2. William Tennent Sr.
   3. Gilbert Tennent
   4. Samuel Davies
   5. Samuel Blair's funeral sermon in 1746
5. Learn evangelistic endeavors in the Middle Colonies by William Robinson, particularly the Revival of 1743 for American Indians (David Brainerd), blacks, and Quakers.
6. The Holy Club and Henry Scougal's book *The Life of God in the Soul of Man*.

Three Affective Domains

1. Feel the human and family affection concerns of the "lonely but not alone" position of William Robinson in America.
2. Empathize and appreciate William Robinson's anecdotal examples of humility.
3. Experience the ecstasy of piety and personal sanctification of William Robinson's autobiographical letter.

INTRODUCTION

Trifecta

What makes evangelist William Robinson's letter of 1741 significant is that it hits the trifecta of historical documents.

1. You have very important persons, George Whitfield and William Robinson
2. They are describing significant events, the Great Awakening's *firepower.*
3. It occurs during extraordinary times: a smallpox epidemic and the terrible snows of 1720–1722. Even during these times of extremely severe weather, they didn't fail to detour the Most High God.

Jonathan Edwards has been credited by some as having started the uniting of the revivals in the colonies, prior to the Great Awakening, to his own congregation in Northampton, Massachusetts, and on July 8, 1741, in Enfield, Connecticut, he said, "Sinners in the hand of an angry God."[2]

---

[2] Public domain.

PROLOGUE

Light the Fire Again! The Eighteenth Century's Bright Light for the Twenty-First Century's Darkness

Thirty-seven years before America's birthday, in 1739, a heretofore mostly unknown American evangelist stood shoulder to shoulder as a peer with a well-known evangelistic team of the Great Awakening. Many American historians are familiar with the eighteenth century and the famous names George Whitfield and the William Tennent family, but there is scant information about a fervent, effective, and successful colleague named William Robinson.

Samuel Davies, the fourth president of Princeton University, was mentored by William Robinson and was the beneficiary of William Robinson's library. Davies said the following of William Robinson in a letter written while he was a minister in Hanover, Virginia, to a Mr. Bellamy in New England on June 18, 1751:

> Probably Mr. Robinson, during the short period of his life, was the instrument in the conversion of as many souls as any minister who ever lived in this country. The only circumstance relating to his person which has come down [in other words—no journals, letters, or written sermons until now!] is

that he was blind of one eye; so that he was called by some "the one-eyed Robinson."[3]1

The biography of an eighteenth-century spiritual light in no way makes a pretense of being an exhaustive chronological account of the American colonies' Great Awakening. It is, rather, a very narrow focus on one of the unknown Great Awakening's key associate itinerant evangelists, William Robinson. This biography is a thrilling unveiling of brand-new and long-lost excerpts of a letter from William Robinson written to a cousin in England. This ten-page letter reflects personal information about his family, facts of his ministry, and an eyewitness to the mighty workings of God in the Great Awakening. The letter itself is in its entirety destined to be available to all theological libraries. Currently, there have been discussions with Barry Driver at Southwestern Baptist Theological Seminary and Steven Crocco at Princeton University regarding its placement.

Robinson's letter is written from Trenton, New Jersey, on June 16, 1741, to his unnamed cousin in an undisclosed location in England. It is possible the location was William Robinson's family home in Carlisle. The letter is in response to his cousin's letter, written to him and mailed from England on April 10, 1740.

The letter came into my possession while my wife and I were in England as pastor of four Baptist churches from 2007 to 2010. The churches were Bishop Auckland Baptist Church, Crook Baptist Church, Hamsterley Baptist Church, and Wolsingham Baptist Church. While I was cleaning the building, there were some books

---

[3] Samuel Davies, *Letters from the Rev. Samuel Davies* (London, 1757), 110–11.

and papers headed for disintegration and disposal at Hamsterley Baptist Church, from whence I happily rescued this letter.

The good news is that the majority of the letter is mostly intact after 271 years. However, there remains one partial page on which there is a brief but significant discussion on the two predecessors to Princeton University, the Log College and the College of New Jersey. Of note is that William Robinson is one of the seven to ten known principal graduates of William Tennent Sr.'s Log College.

As will be evident in this biography, William Robinson was a peer with George Whitfield, William Tennent Sr., Gilbert Tennent, William Tennent Jr., John Tennent, and Charles Tennent. In addition, we will see the very high review of William Robinson from his Great Awakening colleagues, Samuel Davies, Gilbert Tennent, Samuel Blair, and some eighteenth-century extant churchmen. William Robinson is not only an eyewitness to the years of the 1739–1746 during the Great Awakening but is also vitally involved as an inspired and anointed itinerant evangelist.

Finally, the addition of the knowledge on William Robinson is valuable both informationally and directionally to the extant historical record for the years 1739–1746. Particularly, we will see that this letter from June 16, 1741, chronicles what some scholars have viewed as the heart of the Great Awakening (1739–1741). The value of firsthand knowledge is inestimable. In regard to this, C. S. Lewis once said, "First-hand knowledge [*sic*] of great authors is not only worth acquiring more than secondhand knowledge, but is [*sic*] also usually much easier; and, more difficult to acquire."[4] What C. S. Lewis meant is that firsthand knowledge is spot-on with the facts

---

[4] *Introduction to Athanasius* (Crestwood, NY: St. Vladimir Seminary, 1993).

but admittedly more difficult to acquire because of the scarcity of eyewitnesses.

With this revelation of a significant evangelist of the Great Awakening, I was asked to be a program presenter for the American Theological Library Association (ATLA) conference in Scottsdale, Arizona (June 27–30, 2012), which was well attended. The presentation was only a precursory biography of one of the terrific itinerate evangelists of the Great Awakening in the colonies, William Robinson. Apart from the ten-page letter, there is scant information regarding Mr. Robinson. This letter is personal, and it chronicles much of the results of his preaching and his association with Reverend George Whitfield, Gilbert Tennant, and other leaders of the Great Awakening.

I pray you will be enlightened and inspired by this book. It discusses the spiritual light of the eighteenth century for the twenty-first century's darkness regarding an evangelist to the Great Awakening in the 1741 letter of William Robinson, who by all accounts was one of Jesus Christ's firebrands. He struck a spark that will kindle a twenty-first-century awakening, and our Lord Jesus Christ will raise up a firebrand for the modern times to shine in a dark place.

WILLIAM ROBINSON'S KNOWN EDUCATION

The Founding of Log College

Soon after 1726, when William Tennent became the pastor of the Presbyterian Church on Little Neshaminy Creek in Bucks County, Pennsylvania, he began in earnest to educate his three younger sons and some other young men who wanted to study for the ministry. For several years Tennent trained students in his home and then in a nearby cabin that he built. The students lived with William and Katherine Tennent and found themselves completely incorporated into the Tennent family—studying, working, eating, and worshiping.

Because he established the Log College, William Tennent is often credited with beginning something new. Archibald Alexander called Tennent's school "the first seminary" in which students were trained for the ministry within the Presbyterian Church. Gary Schnittjer claims that "Tennent's private ministerial academy was the earliest documented in the American colonies." But Tennent was simply acting within a well-established tradition when he began his "college."

He was familiar with the local academies in his native Ireland and in Scotland and with the pattern of ministerial preparation in America.

William Tennent's school continued for less than twenty years. It never had more than one part-time teacher. Only about twenty young men studied at the Log College. Yet Leonard Trinterud calls the founding of this little school "the most important event in colonial Presbyterianism." In 1889 a New York newspaper stated that "what the landing of the Pilgrims was to Congregationalism in this country, the founding of the Log College has been to Presbyterianism."[5]

One of the Principal Alumni of the Log College

Tennent's students excelled in preaching and in the practical areas of pastoral work. The "character of Gospel laborers," Tennent stressed, "implies that such have a knowledge of the work, and the skill to manage it right." Young George Whitfield wrote that he had never heard "such a searching sermon" as one given by Gilbert Tennent.[6]

Archibald Alexander writes about ten of the principal graduates of the Log College. William Robinson was one of these principals.

> Gary Schnittjer states that Tennent's "distinctive contribution was perhaps what is currently being called 'mentoring' and," Schnittjer explains, "accounts for the effectiveness of the Log College. This method of theological training was not limited to Tennent. Other pastors took in a student or two

---

[5] Alexander, Archibald. *The Log College: Biographical Sketches of William Tennent and Principal Alumni of the Log College* (Birmingham, AL: Solid Ground Christian Books, 1846).

[6] Ibid.

at a time and provided personalized training for them, but Tennent trained a larger number of students for a longer time. He did on a slightly larger and more organized scale what others had done for some time. The important role that mentoring plays in vocational training has become widely recognized today. Thus, 'The Log College way of education,'" asserts Schnittjer, "can serve as a pattern for mentoring as well as academics."[7]

The Princeton Connection

The connection between the Log College, which closed in the early 1740s because of Tennent's age and increasing frailty, and the College of New Jersey, which began in 1746, has often been noted. Chapter 7 in Archibald Alexander's *Log College* is titled "The Log College—The Germ from which Proceeded the College of New Jersey." After the Log College closed, there was no school where the New Side Presbyterians could train their pastors, but this need was quickly addressed, and soon New Side leaders were planning to create a school. "It is noteworthy that the ministers who now exerted themselves in the establishment of the New Jersey College were all friends of the Log College," wrote Archibald Alexander; "and most of them had received their training, both in classical and theological learning, within the walls of this humble institution."[8]

Before the College of New Jersey moved to its permanent location in Princeton in 1756, it existed for a few years on the pattern of the Log College, as an academy headed first by Jonathan Dickinson in

---

[7] Ibid.
[8] Ibid.

Elizabethtown and then by Aaron Burr in Newark (he died in 1757 or 1758). In 1889, James McCosh, former president of Princeton College, wrote, "The Log College was a well among the hills from which a great and beneficent stream has risen. The Tennents and Blairs, were heroes." The college in the wilderness insisted on two great principles, a native ministry and an educated ministry. This led indirectly to the establishment of the college at Princeton.[9]

When Princeton Seminary was founded in 1812, it too claimed to be a successor to the Log College. The Log College was both a college and a theological seminary, but its purpose was the training of ministers. When the General Assembly of the Presbyterian Church decided in 1811 to establish a theological seminary, there was considerable discussion concerning the location of the new school. Not a few people were strongly in favor of placing it on the very site of the Log College.

As Princeton College and Princeton Seminary became the key educational institutions for American Presbyterians, the historic significance of the little school on the banks of Neshaminy Creek in Bucks County, Pennsylvania, was guaranteed.[105]

> There seems to be no written record of the existence of Log College as that which we are describing by any contemporary writer, except in the Journal of Rev. George Whitfield, the celebrated evangelist, who traversed this country several times, preaching everywhere with a popularity and success which have never been equaled until this time. It will be proper,

---

[9] Ibid., "William Robinson's Known Education."

[10] Ibid., Introduction, ix.

therefore, to extract the paragraph which relates to this subject, as he gives the dimensions of the building, and expressly says that it had obtained the name of The College. "The place" says he, "wherein the young men study now, is in contempt called The College. It is a log house, about twenty feet long, and near as many broad; and to me it seemed to resemble the school of the old prophets, for their habitations were mean; and that they sought not great things for themselves is plain from those passages of Scripture, wherein we are told that each of them took them a beam to build them a house: and that at the feast of the sons of the prophets, one of them put on the pot, whilst the others went to fetch some herbs out of the field. All that we can say of most of our universities is, they are glorious without. From this despised place, seven or eight worthy ministers of Jesus have lately been sent forth; more are almost ready to be sent, and the foundation is now laying for the instruction of many others."[11]

The Great Awakening also stimulated a concern for higher education. In 1740, Harvard, William and Mary, Yale (founded 1701) were the only colonial colleges. Leaders elsewhere in the colonies had long expressed an interest in founding colleges, and the revival added to that interest.[12]

---

[11] *George Whitfield's Journals*, 11/22/1739, 354–55.
[12] Mark A. Noll, *Eerdmans' Handbook to Christianity in America* (Grand Rapids, MI: Eerdmans, 1983), 115.

WILLIAM ROBINSON:

THE MAN AND HIS MINISTRY

WILLIAM ROBINSON'S EARLY YEARS IN ENGLAND AND AMERICA'S MIDDLE COLONIES

In England

William Robinson was the son of a Quaker. His father was a man of wealth, and an eminent physician, and was born near Carlisle, England, a little after the beginning of the eighteenth century. William expected to inherit considerable property, not only from his father, but from an aunt in London; but, on going to London to visit that aunt, he greatly overstayed the time which had been allowed him, and plunged into the dissipations of the city, thereby contracting debts which his aunt refused to pay, and which he knew would excite the indignation of his father. Being unable to remain in London, and fearing to return home, he resolved to seek his fortune in America. To this proposal his aunt gave a reluctant consent and furnished him with a small sum.[13]

In America

On his arrival in this country, he found it necessary to engage in some active business for his support; and he betook himself to teaching a school in Hopewell, New Jersey, within the bounds of the Presbytery of New Brunswick. It seems probable that he taught a classical school in the State of Delaware also; for Samuel Davies, whose parents resided in Delaware, was, at one time, one of his pupils. We hear nothing of his erratic tendencies after he left England, and his habits, from that time became hither, seem to have been those of a correct and sober man.[14]

---

[13] William B. Sprague, *Annals of the American Pulpit; or Commemorative Notices of Distinguished Alumni of the Log College, together with An Account of the Revivals of Religion under their Ministry in the 18th Century* (Birmingham, AL: Solid Ground Christian, 1846), Mr. Davies's letter to Mr. Bellamy of New England, p. 193.
[14] Ibid.

WILLIAM ROBINSON'S CONVERSION

He had been engaged in his school for some time, before his mind was practically directed to the subject of religion; and the manner in which this was finally brought about, was somewhat remarkable. As he was riding at a late hour one evening, when the moon and stars were shining with uncommon brightness, he was saying to himself,—*"How transcendently glorious must be the author of all this beauty and grandeur!"* And the thought struck him with irresistible force—*"But what do I know of this God? Have I ever sought his favour, or made Him my friend?"* This impression never left him, until he found peace and joy in believing.[15]

Concerning the early history of this successful evangelist very little is known. The only account which the writer has met with, is that

---

[15] Ibid.

found in a note in the "Life of the Rev. Dr. Rodgers," by the Rev. Dr. Miller.[16]

Mr. Robinson was never married, and it is believed he had no relatives in this country. As far as it appears, he never printed anything or left any of his writings to be a memorial in posterity of his fervent piety and evangelical spirit. It is not even known where his body rests, but his glorious Master, whom he served so faithfully in the gospel, will know where to find it when he shall come to resuscitate the bodies of his saints.[17]

[9]ibid
[10]ibid

---

[16] Ibid.
[17] Ibid.

GILBERT TENNENT'S REVIVAL REPORT OF EVANGELISTS TO GEORGE WHITFIELD (12/13/1740–03/17/1741)

In the letter of Gilbert Tennent to George Whitfield, we find that he refers to Mr. Robinson's successful endeavors in New York: "And many, I hear, have been awakened by the labours of Mr. Robinson, in New York government."

> But it will be satisfactory to hear Mr. Gilbert Tennent's own account ... addressed to Mr. Whitfield ... "Very dear brother ... the work of God spreads more and more. My brother William has had remarkable success this winter (1740–1741) at Burlington. Mr. John Cross has had remarkable success at Staten Island; and many, I hear, have been awakened by the labours of Mr. Robinson, in New York government. Mr. Mills has had remarkable success in Connecticut, particularly at New Haven.

And I hear Mr. Blair has had remarkable success in Pennsylvania.[18]

The excerpt from Gilbert Tennent's revival report to George Whitfield was Tennent's evangelistic campaign in Boston (1740–1741), with his revival focus on Boston, Charlestown, Cambridge, New Haven, Milford, and twenty other towns to which the revival had extended. This period of revival was from December 13, 1740 to March 1741.

---

[18] Ibid.

DISCOVERED LETTER OF WILLIAM ROBINSON: THE MAN AND HIS MINISTRY, 1740–1741

The following reportage is autobiographical and comes exclusively from the letter William Robinson wrote in his discovered letter to his cousin in England in June 1741. He marks his ministry in the fall 1740 extending into late May or June 1741. "About two days ago I received yours ... bearing the date April the 10th 1740. It had been received by the Postmaster in Trenton about six months before I returned from where I had been sent to preach last fall ʿNew York)."

In the letter, he says,

> Many are the thousands Brot to Christ and on the way Children, youth & aged persons, rich and poor, Black and White, tis no Great Matter here to preach unto FIVE Thousand People, for my brethren (Tennents and Principals of Log College) to preach 3–4 or 5 times a day. My constitution is weak yet I've preached 10 times a week some

others twenty, the Power of God is wonderful, Hundreds sometimes cry out in Congregations under a deep sense of their Miserable Lost and Christless Estate, whole assemblies are turned into Bochims (Weepers). Floods of tears appears over Congregations, Hundreds again are Melted with the Love of Christ, faint away and die almost in Pangs of Divine Love."

I cannot think but that it equals or Surpasses the Apostles days. Wherever it comes, People are filled with zeal for God, and others with bitter Rage as word is sent among them. Indeed there wants nothing but the Countenance of Government for a bloodstained persecution If these Barriers of Liberty were removed ...

Before I became a minister, I am apt to think your Labour for Christ will not be fruitless. Neither in the same lauded method, certainly the Lord has blessed the feeble Endeavors of many in this land in a Private Capacity for much good to their friends and neighbors, nay much of the work is thus carried on as Well as Begun ...

Mr. Robinson, in his letter written on June 16, 1741, to his cousin, states that "He was sent forth from New Brunswick Presbytery for his first evangelism assignment in the Fall of 1740 and only returned in June, 1741." Mr. Robinson also refers in his letter to when he was licensed to preach and admitted to the Presbytery: "'Tis above a year since I was licensed to preach and admitted into the Presbytery." Thus, this would put the origin of his ministry's commencement in April–May 1740 by his account. However, we have more precise information: "on the 27th of May [sic] 1740 following, he was licensed to preach the gospel. On the 4th of August, 1741, he was ordained at New Brunswick sine titulo."[19]

---

[19] Archibald Alexander, *The Log College*, 32.

TRANSLATION OF WILLIAM ROBINSON'S LETTER TO HIS COUSIN IN ENGLAND, JUNE 16, 1741

Very Dear [?] Cousin, Pensilvania June 16th 1741

About two days ago I received yours inclosed in Robert Stoddarts bearing date Aprill the 10th 1740. It had been received by the Postmaster in Trenton for me above six months till I returned from where I had been sent to preach last fall. Your letter seems to confirm what I had Entertained hope of Respecting you, now some years, I think a more Dear Affection arises in my breast towards you then that substisting between those under Natural and Relative Bonds only I hope my very dear Cousin, our Lord has made us nearer by Grace than by nature, Nay has not the same Rich and sovereign Grace Encircled and embraced us both in its arms. I trust wee are members of the same body, United to the same Glorious head, Partakers of the same Bread Nurished from the same fountain, Children of one Father, of one Family, not sit together in Heavenly

Places in Christ Jesus, and shall I trust ever Be with him, oh how is my Poor soul refreshed, my Bowels are indeed moved, within me, as these words drop from my Pen, Oh how I long to Embrace you Dear Cousin.

But that God who has separated me from my fathers House and Brethren, has Put a wide Distance between us at Present & I cannot Repine, Nay I bless him for all his Providential Disposals towards me. However I shall rejoice to see your face in the Flesh, and Tho This Perhaps may never be granted, wee shall anon. I hope meet at our Lords Throne in the Kingdom of Glory above and never be separated any more, and now Whilst wee are in the way Lets look unto our Glorious Forerunner wee must live by Faith as just as we have always done in their Peregrination through this strange Land below, oh let our Eye be Immovably Fixed here upon the amiable and Immaculate Righteousness wrot by an Incarnate God, his active and Passive Obedience, oh what splendid and unfading Raiment is here For us, oh let us ever Muse upon those and surely the fire of love will not only Kindle but burn yea break forth into a violent flame.

Lets look upwards and behold our Immanuel Enthroned in the most sublime Majesty, Glory & Dignity, manageing the Reigns of Government over the whole Creation see his Transendant Beauties & uncreated glories He's indeed altogether lovely, oh the Radiant Charms & Inimitable Excellence that dwell upon his countence, He has not his fellow upon Earth nor his Equal among the angels oh what a plenitude, nay what an immense & unfathomable ocean of grace Mercy & Love is here behold his unutterable sufficiency the infinite wisdom Power & unsearchable Compassion & Goodness of this Blessed King & Meadiator. O Let him dwell upon our souls day & night as a Pomander of Myrrhe between our Breasts, O Lets ever be ravaged with his beauty, satisfied & Transported with his love, Does views of our own weakness and ignorance Invade us the number Power & Policy of our Enemies, Here's a Glorious Refuge, wisdom & strength to guide & Protect us, Defeat & Confound them, Does swelling & insuperable mountains of Temptations Discouragement & Guilt Rise Before us Lo hear's an Ocean of Grace Mercy & Love to sinck overwhelm & bury the Loftiest—

Heads of them all, Does darkness overspread us Here's the Fountain of Light, if deadness here's Life, does Corruption stir and boil over, look this way hence comes a calm, lo here's the Fountain to wash in, when ever wee turn one Eye upon our selves our Guilt, our Blemishes, our vileness, our Loathsomeness. Let the other be fixed upon Christ Let faith Ever be stirring, ever on work, this will make our spiknard Cast forth its smell, this will draw forth all our graces in their Proper Order & Place. Increase Their vigor & strength bring life Comfort & Joy Down into our souls and preserve it there, this Thro the Influences of the Divine Spirit will lift us above the world, bring us to an holy Content of Terrene Enjoyments, Enouble & Greeaten our minds Transform us into the Divine image, Triumph over our Enemies and come at last laden with huge treasures of the precious gain & merchandise of Grace into the Haven of Endless Glory—

Oh may wee thus live a life of Faith, thus looking unto & leaning upon our beloved, till wee be Elapsed in the Embraces of his Boundless and Eternal love above, but alas whether shall I run, oh that my Relations and my Poor sister might be visited with the salvation of God, oh that they might be Regenerated & Ingrafted by faith into Christ may

Infinite Love Pity them so they lay in their blood oh that God would drop down his Love into their hearts and Infuse spiritual life into them—

I'm glad to hear of your Brother Garthorns Family, the religious family you have married into. I am not of your opinion in Religion, But circumstantial differences are nothing with me. I desire and hope I do Love unfaintedly all that Loves Christ. I can embrace them as Brethren howsoever they be as to sect. This creates no alienation of affection in me. I bless God he's given me a Catholick spirit, a spirit not tied up & Restricted to Presbyterians or any denomination so shoud be glad to Cultivate a Correspondence with your Brother—

Mr. Whitfield has informed us of the situation of the Religion in England tis I suppose like to grow & spread in the Power of it, and I pray God it may Reach Cumberland also, I intimated to you some Presages of the Increase of Christs Kingdom in this Land which have not failed, here has been such Surprising Effusions of God's spirit in the ministry Especially under Mr. Whitfield & our new Brunswick Presbytery in which are the Famous Tennents my dear brethren, that all New England, the Provinces of York, the Jersies, Pensilvania, and Maryland are filled with Convinced & Converted souls, many are the thousands Brot to Christ and on the way Children, youth & aged persons, rich & poor Black & White, tis no Great Matter here to preach unto Five Thousand People, for my Brethren to preach 3-4 or 5 times a day. My Constitution is but weak yet I've Preached 10 times a week some others twenty, the Power of God is wonderful, Hundreds sometimes cry out In Congregations under a deep sense of their Miserable Lost and Christless Estate, whole assemblies are turned into Bochims. Floods of tears appears over Congregations, Hundreds again are Melted with the Love of Christ, Faint away and die almost in Pangs of Divine Love, I cannot think but what it Equals or Surpasses the apostles days wherever itt comes People are filled with zeal for God, and others with bitter Rage, as word is sent among them. Indeed there wants nothing but the Countenance of the Government for a bloodstained Persecution If these Barriers of Liberty were Removed an awful sceen would I believe directly Ensue however the more the work is opposed the more it grows & spreads and indeed itt Increases daily, tis now above a year Since I was Licensed to preach and admitted into the Presbytry (said—"sd") above I cannot tell what great things God has done for Me, what honors conferred on me a poor Ignorant wretch oh that I may be humble & thankful—

Time will not my many avocations will not suffer me to gratify your desires Respecting a Relation of my Experience at Present, Inform Robert Stoddart I thank him for his Kind letter and Kind offices I have not nor ever had any Resentments against him I desire his happiness I beg him & you and any other that has any acquaintance with true and vital Piety, would Exert your selves in Essaying the advancement of Christs honour and the good of souls. Let not Different sentiments about some things hinder mutual Endeavors this way Dear Cousin nay Brother Labour to Promote meetings of Prayer & Religious Conferences among you and Perhaps God may own it above what you think or imagine I wish my Dear Cousin and old Friend Robt. would do the same about him, if God has given you knowledge & grace above others use it for the Glory of the giver thereof. I know the Lord Blessed my attempts for the Conversion of many this way—

Before I came to be a minister, I am apt to think your Labour for Christ will not be fruitless neither in the same laudable method, certainly the Lord has Blessed the feeble Endeavours of many in this Land in a Private Capacity for much good to their friends and neighbors, nay much of the work is thus Carried on as well as Begun oh, try try for the Lords sake, send my very Dear Love to my sister & brother, warn them of their danger and the necessity of a new heart, and the real Knowledge of the saving faith in Christ Jesus. I want directions to write to her, my love to all friends, I go over Sundry Provinces as an Itenerant and am like to do so from the order of my Presbytry. The best way therefore will be to Direct for me to the care of Mr. Thomas Noble in New York. Merchant who's a noted Gentleman and an Israelite Indeed; twill come this way most safely & speedily to me where ever I may I am yours Dear Cousin, and C. Wm. Robinson

P.S. The colleges of New England are now Replenished with young men of quite a different stamina.

They were about a year ago, there's not above Eight Persons in both but whats Either convicted or converted chiefly by Brother Whitfield & Mr. Gilbert Tennent's Preaching, Salt being thus cast into the Fountain the streams are like to be sweet, and Promises yet greater things in this Land I cannot but think the Thousand years are beginning. For Christs Reigning by the Gospel over the Nations tho before in the universal the witnesses are like to be Slain a Short Time of Persecution will be on the faithful, Many Quakers are truly Converted Baptized and Received the sacrament of the Lords supper. Many are Persecuted by their Parents Cast out of their houses and familys But all severities avail nothing—

Excuse my brevity and confusion & let me hear from you & beg my sister to write & Let me know about her soul affairs—Let P. Robert write, you write and spare not __ Pray for us __

I've writ as fast as possible—

Soon after his ordination, he determined to go to visit the "lost sheep of the house of Israel," that is the distant and dispersed settlements of Presbyterians in the states south of New Jersey … on the frontier of Pennsylvania that were greatly infested by the hostile incursions of the Indians, which induced them to turn their attention to the Western parts of Virginia and North Carolina. In some instances whole congregations, driven from their homes by the brutes, removed in a body with their ministers to a region less exposed to the excursions of their murderous foes. They generally landed in New Castle or Philadelphia and then proceeded to the interior of the country. There were Presbyterians from the north of Ireland, between the years 1720 and 1730, had come over to America in large numbers.[20]

The valley between the Blue Ridge and the North mountain—fine limestone farming country—was first occupied by these Irish Presbyterians; the Germans, who now possess a large part of this fertile region, came in afterward. In many places, all along the frontier were small groups of Presbyterians who were entirely destitute of the public means of grace.

Mr. Robinson's ministry benefited from the starting point with the Ulster Scots Ireland immigration of Presbyterians. In his letter as well as elsewhere, they are referred to as "Israelites."

---

[20] Archibald Alexander, *The Log College*, 32.

WILLIAM ROBINSON'S
MINISTRY, 1741–1742

For the most part, all of these years of ministry of William Robinson are drawn upon meager biographical and anecdotal historical data.

> To these scattered sheep, Mr. Robinson directed his benevolent attention … In another respect he resembled Paul for he went forward … and as it would seem, without even inquiring whether the laws of the colonies into which he was going would allow itinerant preachers to pass though the land (1741–1742).

WILLIAMS ROBINSON'S
MINISTRY, 1742–1743

The next winter, he was sent as an evangelist by the Presbytery of Newcastle, in consequence of an earnest request from the people to visit the Presbyterian settlements in the Valley of the Shenandoah; on the south side of the James River, in Virginia; and in the numerous settlements of North Carolina, on the Haw. Accordingly, he had penetrated but a short day's journey into the Old Dominion and reached the town of Winchester, when he was arrested by the sheriff of Orange County. It appeared that he had transgressed the laws of the colony, and a mittimus was made out by the magistrate to send him to Williamsburg, the then seat of government, to answer to before he had proceeded far. However, the sheriff, finding that he was evidently a sensible and well-disposed man, released him and suffered him to pursue his mission unmolested. He passed the winter in Carolina and, in consequence of imprudent exposures, contracted a disease from which he never recovered. It is believed the disease was smallpox, and he was blinded in one eye and was given the nickname "One-eyed Robinson."[21]

Mr. Robinson proceeded along the valley, everywhere finding new settlements of Presbyterians, until he reached the waters of the James River. There was an old man who was among the first settlers of the country round about Lexington, then called the Forks, and the man said he had heard Mr. Robinson preach in that settlement soon after it was formed. But the inhabitants in the valley did not extend any farther to the southwest, so he returned and crossed the Blue Ridge at Rockfish Gap. He proceeded to the south, across the country, until he reached Cub Creek, then in Lunenburg, now Charlotte. Here, he found a pretty large settlement of Presbyterians, and he stopped and preached. Here as in all other places, his ministry was attended by the Spirit of God; sinners were awakened and converted, and the people of God were greatly strengthened and comforted.

When Robinson was young, he conversed with an old man who was living in this settlement at the time and was afterward an elder in the church organized there. His name was Robert Weakly, and he was born in Pennsylvania. Though brought up among the opposers of the revival, Weakly was led by curiosity to hear the Rev. Samuel Blair preach, and he was brought under deep conviction, and, after many trials, he hoped to a sound conversion. From this time, he connected himself with the "New Lights," as they were called. This man had moved into Halifax County late in life, where he had no opportunity of attending the Lord's Supper in his own church, and he was debarred from the communion by the Baptists among whom he lived unless he would submit to be immersed. He was at length induced to go down with them under the water. Though he was

---

[21] Ibid. 195–96.

nominally a Baptist, his heart was as truly Presbyterian as ever. He was a man of eminent and long-tried piety, and he had a good report from all of every name, whether in the church or out of it.

This same elderly man informed me that under Mr. Robinson's first sermon, a remarkable conversion of a part-Indian man, one of the wickedest of men, had taken place under unusual circumstances. When notice was given to his family of a sermon preached by a traveling preacher, his wife wished to go, but he positively forbade her, but said he would go himself. His name was David Austin. When the congregation had collected, he was seen lying outside the assembly under a tree asleep. And thus he lay until the preacher took his text, which he uttered in a thundering voice, "Awake, thou that sleepiest." Austin sprang to his feet as if pierced with a dart, and fixing his eyes on the preacher, never removed them, but drew nigher and nigher to the stand, until at the close he was observed standing at the preacher's feet, and the tears streaming from his eyes. After a few days of pungent conviction, he received comfort by faith in Christ, and became one of the most eminent Christians in all the land. His talent for administering consolation to distressed consciences was so well known that he was sent for as far as thirty miles to converse with a lady under spiritual darkness and distress of mind. I have heard a pious old mother say that she had heard Mr. Davies, Dr. Waddel, and the Smiths converse on religion, but she never heard anyone whom she found so much comfort in hearing as old David Austin.[22]

It is highly commendable as an insight to the giftedness of Rev. William Robinson that when William Tennent Sr., one of his highly respected mentors and the head of the Log College, retired due to poor physical health in 1742 from the Presbyterian church on Little Neshaminy Creek in Bucks County, Pennsylvania, Rev. Robinson received a call to Neshaminy as Tennent's successor in 1743.

> In the year 1742, we find the following minutes on the records of the Presbytery. "Mr. WILLIAM TENNENT, SR., gave into Presbytery a paper, setting forth his inability, by reason of advanced age, to discharge the work of the ministry unto the congregation of Neshaminy, over which for diverse years he had been overseer – desiring the Presbytery to grant to said congregation of Neshaminy such supplies as they can." We find his name enrolled among the members of the New Brunswick Presbytery in the following year (1743) … for in the same year a call was presented to Mr. William Robinson, which he declined.[23]

William Robinson declined this honorable pastoral opportunity and continued on with a most successful itinerant Evangelistic ministry in which he felt the most called to exercise his gifts.

---

[22] Ibid., 195–96.

[23] William B. Sprague, *Annals of the American Pulpit*, 94–95.

WILLIAMS ROBINSON'S
MINISTRY, 1743–1746

On his return from Carolina, he preached with great effect to the Presbyterian settlements in Charlotte, Prince Edward, Campbell, and Albemarle Counties. Here he was waited upon by a deputation that persuaded him, instead of pursuing his contemplated route to the head of the Shenandoah, to return to Hanover, Virginia. The people on whose behalf his services were solicited were far from being agreed in their religious views; some of them had reached the point of denying not only the efficacy but also the expediency of good works, and they doubted whether it was right to pray because prayer could not alter the divine purposes. The delegates who waited upon him, having heard him preach, before extending to him an invitation to return with them, were somewhat divided in opinion concerning his doctrines. They finally gave him a cordial invitation in the name of the congregations. He at first declined, but their importunity at length prevailed, and he made his arrangements to visit Hanover.

On his arrival at Hanover, several prominent individuals had an interview with him, and examined his testimonials, and satisfied themselves in regard to his views of Christian doctrine and practice, and the measures which he proposed to adopt. He submitted to their examination with the utmost meekness and readiness and led them to form high hopes in regard to the success of his labours. He preached to them, for the first time, on Sabbath, July 6, 1743; and it was the first sermon from a Presbyterian minister ever heard in Hanover County. He continued preaching for four successive days; during which the congregation regularly increased, and the impression became constantly deeper. An individual, who was present, giving an account of this series of exercises, seven years after, says—"here is reason to believe there was as much good done by these four sermons, as by all the sermons preached in these parts before or since." And he adds—"Before Mr. Robinson left us, he successfully endeavoured to correct some of our mistakes, and to bring us to carry on the worship of God more regularly at our meetings. After this, we met to read good sermons, and began and concluded with prayer and singing of Psalms, which, till then, we had omitted.[24]

Mr. Robinson, having passed four days, labouring publicly and privately among these people, was constrained to take his departure, in order to meet other engagements; and besides, it began to be rumoured that measures were about to be taken to arrest him as an itinerant. The people, partly to compensate him for his arduous labours, and partly to testify their gratitude towards him, made him a handsome present in money; but he refused to receive it; and when they urged it upon him, he still persevered in his refusal, believing

---

[24] Ibid.

that the peculiar circumstances of the case would not justify him in any other course. The committee to whom the matter was entrusted, being still resolved to carry their point, put it into the hands of a gentleman with whom he was to lodge the night before leaving the county, with instructions that he should deposit it privately in his saddle-bags, not doubting that when he found it there after his departure, he would appropriate it to his own use. This was accordingly done; but, in the morning, when Mr. Robinson came to lift his saddlebags, he found them much heavier than usual, and, on opening them, immediately discovered the cause. He smiled at the benevolent artifice, and said, "I see you are resolved I shall have your money; I will take it; but, as I have told you before, I do not need it; I have enough, nor will I appropriate it to my own use; but there is a young man of my acquaintance, of promising talents and piety, who is now studying with a view to the ministry; but his circumstances are embarrassing; he has not funds to support and carry him on without much difficulty; this money will relieve him from his pecuniary difficulties: I will take charge of it, and appropriate it to his use; and, as soon as he is licensed, we will send him to visit you; it may be that you may now, by your liberality, be educating a minister for yourselves." The young man here referred to was Samuel Davies, afterwards the illustrious President Davies of Princeton. Mr. Robinson applied the money as he had promised; and, in due time, Mr. Davies went to Hanover,—chiefly it is said, in consideration of his peculiar obligations to the people, and remained there ten years, making so broad and deep a mark in the character of the community, that time has done little to efface it.[25]

---

[25] Ibid.

Mr. Robinson's labours, during this tour, were arduous and unremitted, and withal eminently successful. His health, after this, visibly declined; but still he kept at his work, being employed part of the time in the State of New York, and part of the time in Maryland;—and a rich blessing seems everywhere to have attended his labours. Mr. (afterwards President) Davies renders the following testimony concerning him:—

1. In Maryland also there has been a considerable revival, (shall I call it?) or first plantation of religion.

2. In Kent County and in Queen Anne's, a number of careless sinners have awakened and hopefully brought to Christ. The work was begun, and mostly carried on, by the instrumentality of that favoured man, Mr. Robinson, whose success, whenever I reflect upon it, astonishes me. Oh, he did much in a little time; and who would not choose such an expeditious pilgrimage through this world! There are in these places a considerable congregation, and they have made repeated efforts to obtain a settled minister.
But the most glorious display of Divine grace in Maryland has been in and about Somerset County. It began, I think, in 1745, by the ministry of Mr. Robinson, and was afterwards carried on by several ministers who preached transiently there.[26]

---

[26] Ibid., 93–95.

REVIVAL OF 1743 WITH EVANGELIST WILLIAM ROBINSON

A remarkable attention to religion in the county of Hanover existed at this time, without the aid of the ministry. Some persons from that place were on a visit to Cub Creek when Mr. Robinson, on his way to Carolina, visited that settlement, then called the Caldwell Settlement. Those people gave an account upon their return of the preacher they had heard. Upon hearing this account, the serious people of Hanover inquired at what time Mr. Robinson expected to return from Carolina to Cub Creek, and they immediately resolved to send two of their number to meet him at the time specified. It so happened, however, that the information received was not correct, for when the messengers arrived at Cub Creek, they found to their disappointment that he had passed several days before. Determined not to go back without him, they pursued after him through a very rugged, mountainous country and overtook him at Rockfish, at the foot of the Blue Ridge.

Upon hearing the state of things in Hanover, Mr. Robinson did not hesitate to go with the men, but in order to reach the place before the Sabbath, it became necessary to ride one whole night. When he arrived, the leaders of the dissenting congregation were much perplexed and concerned lest his doctrines should not accord with those which from books they had imbibed. Therefore, before he was introduced to the congregation, they took him into a private room and asked him his opinion of such works as Luther on the Galatians, Boston, and Bunyan. When he expressed the warmest approbation, they were delighted above measure. But it will be gratifying to the reader to see the whole of the letter which Mr. Davies wrote to Mr. Bellamy, in which the narrative of Mr. Robinson's visit to Hanover is contained. It shall be here inserted.

The following is a letter from Mr. Davis, minister of Hanover, Virginia, to Mr. Bellamy of Bethlehem in New England.

Rev. and Dear Sir:—If the publication of a narrative of the rise, progress, and present situation of religion in Virginia, may not only gratify good people, but (as you give me reason to hope) animate their prayers for us, and also encourage preachers to come into these parts, I should charge myself with a criminal neglect if I refused to publish the marvelous works of the Lord among us. I hope I may observe without the umbrage of calumny what is but too evident to serious people of all denominations among us, that religion has been and in most parts of the colony still is in a very low state. A surprising negligence in attending public worship, and an equal surprising levity and unconcernedness in those that attend. Family religion a rarity, and a solemn concern about eternal things, a greater. Vices of various kinds triumphant, and even a form of godliness not common. But universal fame makes it needless for me to enlarge on this disagreeable subject. Before the revival in 1743, there were a few who were awakened, as they have told me, either by their own serious reflections, suggested and enforced by divine energy, or on reading some authors of the last century, particularly Bolton, Baxter, Flavel, Bunyan. There was one Mr. Samuel Morris who had for some time been very anxious about his own salvation, who, after obtaining blessed relief in Christ, became zealous for the salvation of his neighbours, and very earnest to use means to awaken them. This was the tendency of his conversation; and he also read to them such authors as had been most useful to himself, particularly Luther on the Galatians, and his Table Discourses, and several pieces of honest Bunyan's. By these means some of his neighbours were made more thoughtful about their souls; but the concern was not very extensive. I have prevailed on my good friend just now named, who was the principal private instrument of promoting the late work, and therefore well acquainted with it, to write me a narrative of its rise and progress and this, together with what he and others have told me, I shall present to you without any material alterations.

In the year 1740, Mr. Whitfield had preached at Williamsburgh, at the invitation of Mr. Blair, their late commissary. But we being fifty miles distant from Williamsburgh, he left the colony before we had an opportunity of hearing him. But in the year 1743, a young man from Scotland had got a book of his sermons preached in Glasgow, and taken from his mouth in short hand, which, after I had read with great benefit, I invited my neighbours to come and hear it; and the plainness and fervency of these discourses being attended with the power of the Lord, many were convinced of their undone condition, and constrained to seek deliverance with the greatest solicitude. A considerable number met to hear these sermons every Sabbath, and frequently on week days. The concern of some was so passionate and violent, that they could not avoid crying out and weeping bitterly. And that when such indications of religious concern were so strange and ridiculous that they could not be occasioned by example or sympathy, and the affectation of them would be so unprofitable an instance of hypocrisy that none could be tempted to it.

Mr. Robinson's dwelling-house at length was too small to contain the people, whereupon we determined to build a meeting-house merely for reading. And having never been used to social extempore prayer, none of us durst attempt it. By this single means several were awakened, and their conduct ever since is a proof of the continuance and happy issue of their impressions. When the report was spread abroad I was invited to several places to read there sermons, at a considerable distance, and by this means the concern was propagated. About this time our absenting ourselves from the established Church, contrary as was alleged, to the laws of the land, was taken notice of, and we were called upon by the court to assign our reasons for it, and to declare what denomination we were of. As we knew but little of any denomination of dissenters except Quakers, we were at a loss what name to assume. At length, recollecting that Luther was a noted reformer and that his books had been of especial service to us, we declared ourselves Lutherans, and thus continued, until Providence sent us the Rev. Mr. William Robinson. This Mr. Robinson was a zealous, laborious minister of Christ, who, by the permission of the Presbytery, took a journey through the new settlements in Pennsylvania, Virginia, and North Carolina. He founded a congregation at Lunenburg. In Amelia, also, a county somewhat nearer us than the former, his labours were extensively blest; and while he was there, some of our people sent him an invitation to come and preach at our reading house. Being satisfied about the soundness of his principles, and being informed that the method of his preaching was awakening, we were very eager to hear him. On the 6th of July, 1743, he preached his first sermon to us from Luke 13:3, and continued with us preaching four days successively. The congregation was large the first day, and vastly increased the three ensuing. 'Tis hard for the liveliest imagination to form an image of the condition of the assembly, on these glorious days of the Son of Man. Such of us as had been hungering for the word before were lost in an agreeable surprise and astonishment, and some could not refrain from publicly declaring their transport.

We were overwhelmed with the thoughts of the unexpected goodness of God in allowing us to hear the gospel preached in a manner that surpassed our hopes. Many that came through curiosity were pricked to the heart, and but few in the numerous assemblies on these four days appeared unaffected. They returned alarmed with apprehensions of their dangerous condition, convinced of their former entire ignorance of religion, and anxiously inquiring what they should do to be saved. And there is reason to believe there was as much good done by these four sermons as by all the sermons preached in these parts before or since. Before Mr. Robinson left us he successfully endeavoured to correct some of our mistakes, and to bring us to carry on the worship of God more regularly at our meetings. After this we met to read good sermons and began and concluded with prayer and singing of psalms, which till then we had omitted. The blessing of God remarkably attended these more private means, and it was really astonishing to observe the solemn impressions begun or continued in many by hearing good discourses read. I had repeated invitations to come to many places round, some of them thirty or forty miles distant, to read. Considerable numbers attended with eager attention and awful solemnity, and several were in a judgment of charity turned to God, and thereupon erected meetinghouses and chose readers among themselves, by which the work was more extensively carried on.

Soon after Mr. Robinson left us, the Rev. Mr. John Blair paid us a visit, and truly he came to us in the fullness of the gospel of Christ. Former impressions were ripened, and new ones made on many hearts.[27]

---

[27] Archibald Alexander, *The Log College*, 206.

WILLIAMS ROBINSON'S 1745 NORTH CAROLINA AND MARYLAND MINISTRY

Mr. Robinson underwent great hardships in North Carolina without much success, by reason of the fewness and savage ignorance of the inhabitants, but the case is now happily altered.

A new congregation, I think upon Pee Dee River, sent a petition lately to our Presbytery for a minister. Besides this, I hear of several other places in North Carolina that are ripening very fast for the gospel. O that the Lord would send forth faithful labourers into his harvest! Mr. Robinson was the instrument of awakening several in Lunenburg and Amelia, with whom I lately spent a fortnight at their earnest desire; and there is a prospect of doing much service were they furnished with a faithful minister.[28]

There was a great stir about religion in Buckingham, a place on the sea-shore, about four years ago, which has since spread and issued

---

[28] Samuel Davies, *Letters from the Rev. Samuel Davies.*

in a hopeful conversion in several instances. They also want a minister. But the most glorious display of divine grace in Maryland has been in and about Somerset county. It began, I think, in 1745, by the ministry of Mr. Robinson, and was afterwards carried on by several ministers that preached transiently there. I was there about two months, when the work was at its height, and I never saw such deep and spreading concern; the assemblies were numerous, though in the extremity of a cold winter,[29] and unwearied in attending the word; and frequently there were very few among them that did not give some plain indications of distress or joy. Oh! these were the happiest days that ever my eyes saw. Since that, the harvest seems over there, though considerable gleanings, I hear are still gathered."[30]

Not only in Hanover, but in all the places Mr. Robinson preached, there were permanent fruits of his labours. The writer, Samuel Davies, has seen and conversed with a number of persons who were brought to serious consideration under the ministry of this successful evangelist. Old John White, who resided near Charlestown in Jefferson County, and who was the father of Jude White of Winchester, was one of Mr. Robinson's great admirers, and I believe brought to the experimental knowledge of the truth under his ministry. Old Mr. Hope, the father of the Rev. Dr. Moses Hope, who was a seceder, informed the writer that he often heard Robinson when he preached at Opekin and Cedar Creek, in Frederick County, and while he admitted that he preached the

---

[29] David McCullough, *John Adams* (Simon & Shuster: 2001), 256. John Adams "had been away from home now for more than a year leaving Abigail to face two winters without him. The first of which had been the most severe in 40 years." Abigail's letter, written in 1780–1781, is referencing the winter of 1740–41. The worst winter would have been in the middle of the Great Awakening.

[30] Ibid.

gospel faithfully and with great zeal, yet he said there was a want of method in his discourses. After Mr. Robinson's return from this interesting tour, he labored in the state of New York with his usual success, and also in some congregations in Maryland, where there was a blessed work of grace under his ministry.[31]

---

[31] Ibid.

WILLIAM ROBINSON'S 1745 DELAWARE MINISTRY

On March 19, 1746, Mr. Robinson was dismissed from the Presbytery of New Brunswick to the Presbytery of New Castle, with a view to his becoming the pastor of the congregation in St. George's (Delaware) congregation, which had been gathered under his labors, in connection with those of Mr. Whitfield. But in the April following, before he had yet been installed over his charge, his earthly course was finished. His funeral sermon was preached on the eighth of the succeeding August by the Rev. Samuel Blair. He bequeathed his library to his friend and beneficiary, the Rev. Samuel Davies. There remains little documentary testimony concerning him, but there is a uniform tradition that he was an eminently devout and benevolent man and one of the most vigorous and effective preachers of his day.

The following anecdote is related on the authority of the late Rev. Dr. Hill of Virginia:

On the night before Mr. Robinson was to preach in Hanover for the first time, he rode late to reach a tavern within some eight or ten miles from the place of preaching. The tavern keeper was a shrewd, boisterous, profane man. When uttering some horrid oaths, Mr. Robinson ventured to reprove him for his profanity; and although it was done in a mild way, the innkeeper gave him a sarcastic look, and said, "Pray, Sir, who are you to take such authority upon yourself?" "I am a minister of the Gospel," says Mr. Robinson. "Then you belie your looks very much," was the reply. (It is said that Mr. Robinson had the smallpox very severely, which had given him a very rough visage, and deprived him of the sight of one of his eyes. It was with reference to his forbidding appearance that the innkeeper seemed to question his ministerial character.) "But" says Mr. Robinson, "if you wish certainly to know whether I am a minister or not, if you will accompany me, you may be convinced by hearing me preach" "I will," says the innkeeper, "if you will preach from a text I will give you." "Let me hear it," says Mr. Robinson, "and if there is nothing unsuitable in it, I will." The waggish innkeeper gave him the passage from the Psalms—*"I am fearfully and wonderfully made."* (Psalm 139:14 NASB). Mr. Robinson agreed that it should be one of his texts. The man was at Mr. Robinson's meeting, and that text was the theme of one of his sermons. Before it was finished, the wicked man was made to feel that he was the monster, and that he was fearfully and wonderfully made. It is said that he became a very pious and useful member of the church—Rev. Dr. Hill of Virginia.

Dr. Alexander says,

> Probably Mr. Robinson, during the short period of his life, was the instrument in the conversion of as many souls as any minister who ever lived in this country. The only circumstance relating to his person which has come down, is, that he was blind of one eye; so that by some he was called "the one-eyed Robinson."[32]

> Mr. Robinson's labours, during this tour, were arduous and unremitted, and withal eminently successful (Hanover, Virginia). His health after this visibly declined.[33]

> He paused the winter in Carolina, and, in consequence of imprudent exposures, contracted a disease from which he never recovered.[34]

> Mr. Robinson underwent great hardships in North Carolina without much success... but the case is happily altered.[35]

---

[32] *Various Denominations: From the Early Settlement of the Country to Close of the Year Eighteen Hundred and Fifty-five*, vol. 3 (New York: Carter, 1858), 93–95.

[33] Ibid., 93.

[34] Archibald Alexander, *The Log College*, Mr. Davies's letter to Mr. Bellamy of New England, 206.

[35] Ibid.

William Robinson says,

> I cannot but think with all this intensity of the earthquake in thousands of lives here in America, that it equals or surpasses the Apostles. In those days, wherever the Holy Spirit came, people were filled with a zeal for God. I would be remiss if I did not report that the enemy has controlled others with bitter rage as God's word is among them - again, just like the Apostles' days.[36]

---

[36] Ibid.

WILLIAM ROBINSON'S DEATH

During the short period of his life, Mr. Robinson probably was the instrument in the conversion of as many souls as any minister who ever lived in this country. The only circumstance relating to his person that we know for sure is that he was blind of one eye, so some called him "the One-eyed Robinson."

Samuel Davies said, "We are also entirely ignorant of the circumstances of his death." This event we know occurred before the year 1751, in which Mr. Davies wrote his letter to Mr. Bellamy, for it is mentioned with grief in that communication. If we are not mistaken, Mr. Davies has celebrated the labors and successes of this servant of God in one of his poems, and Mr. Tennent somewhere speaks of him as "that wonderful man."[37]

---

37 Ibid., 206.

STARTING THE FIRE IN THE EIGHTEENTH CENTURY

Evangelist William Robinson was a principal colleague and graduate of Log College, and he was an evangelist who played a significant role in the Great Awakening with George Whitfield, William Tennent Sr., Gilbert Tennent and his family, and other principal graduates.

For a brief time in the early 1740s, religious events dominated the news in colonial America. Prime newspaper space usually devoted to matters emanating from statehouses contained the latest developments from meetinghouses. Weeklies from Boston to Charleston reported the huge crowds, often numbering in the thousands, who gathered at outdoor preaching services. Observers at those meetings described bizarre behavior including 'Out-Cries, Faintings and Fits' as men and women reacted to frightening depictions of eternal damnation. Reporters noted the presence of persons who had theretofore rarely attended Christian churches.

Joseph Park, minister at Westerly, Rhode Island, recorded that while 'there were not above *ten or twelve* Indians that used to come to Meeting at all, there is now *near an Hundred* that come very constantly.' Others, who had formerly attended worship but paid little attention to sermons, suddenly began to take heed. John Tennent, pastor at Freehold, New Jersey, indicated that many who had previously gone to church 'for their Diversion, viz to hear News or speak to their Trades-Men,' now 'were taken in the Gospel Net.' And concern about religion spread into regions once considered barren of spiritual sensitivities.[38]

In addition,

there are thousands of Blacks in this colony [Baltimore, Maryland], who still continue in the grossest ignorance; and most foolish carelessness about religion, and rank as pagans as when they left the wilds of Africa ... But I think, Sir, my ministry of late has been most successful among them. Two Sundays ago, I had the pleasure of seeing forty of their black faces around the Table of the Lord, who all made a credible profession of Christianity; and, sundry of them with unusual evidences of sincerity.... Last Sunday, I baptized seven or eight adults who had been in catechism for some time ...

---

[38] Samuel Davies, *Letters from the Rev. Samuel Davies*, 110–11.

What was going on is a question that elicited much comment from contemporaries and continues to intrigue historians. Extensive coverage suggests that men and women of the time regarded these unusual occurrences as a major event in mid-eighteenth-century colonial America. Even after war erupted in 1739 between England and Spain, with fighting raging in the Americas, religious news remained on the front pages of colonial newspapers.[39]

The main evangelist of the Great Awakening in the American colonies was George Whitfield. Mr. Whitfield traces his anointing and inspiration in evangelism to a seventeenth-century Puritan piety book.

When I was sixteen years of age, I began to fast twice a week for thirty-six hours together, prayed many times a day, received the sacrament every Lord's day, fasting myself almost to death all the forty days of Lent, during which I made it a point of duty never to go less than three times a day to public worship, besides seven times a day to my private prayers, yet I knew no more that I was to be born again in God, born a new creature in Christ Jesus, than if I were never born at all ... I must bear testimony to my old friend Mr. Charles Wesley; he put a book into my hands, called *The Life of God in*

---

[39] Frank Lambert, *Inventing the Great Awakening* (Oxford: Princeton University Press, 1999), 3.

47

> *the Soul of Man*, whereby God showed me, that I must be born again or be damned.[40]

Charles Wesley gave the book *The Life of God in the Soul of Man* to George Whitfield, and the Holy Spirit lit a fire and experienced "the new birth." God used the author, Henry Scougal, to awaken the man who himself was later known as the Awakener.[41]

William Robinson, while in the company of the Tennents, relates in his letter the nature of his relationship with George Whitfield.

> Mr. Whitfield has informed us of the situation in England tis I suppose like to grow and spread in the power of it, and I pray God it may reach Cumberland also. I intimated to you some Presages of the Increase of Christ's Kingdom in this Land which have not failed. Here has been such Surprising Effusions of God's Spirit in the ministry. Especially under Mr. Whitfield & our New Brunswick Presbytery in which are the famous Tennents, my dear brethren, that all New England, the Provinces of York, the Jersies, Pensilvania, and Maryland are filled with convinced and converted souls, many thousands brought to Christ.

In another portion of the letter, in assessing the students at the Log College and the College of New Jersey, Robinson states, "The colleges of New England are now Replenished with young men of

---

[40] Henry Scougal, *The Life of God in the Soul of Man* (Fearn: Christian Focus, 1996), 4–15.

[41] Ibid.

quite a different stamina … There were about a year ago, there's not above Eight Persons in both but what's either convicted or converted chiefly by Brother Whitfield & Mr. Gilbert Tennent's Preaching. Salt being cast into the Fountain the streams are like to be sweet and Promise yet greater."

Someone makes a spoken evaluation that "the spiritual climate of the 18th Century was muddled in the established churches and malevolent in the secular climate."

The Great Awakening revival, one historian has said,

> changed … the whole tone of English society … The [Anglican] Church was restored to new life and activity. Religion carried to the hearts of the people a fresh spirit of moral zeal, while it purified our literature and our manners. A new philanthropy reformed our prisons, infused clemency and wisdom into our penal laws, abolished the slave-trade, and gave the first impulse to popular education.

Another historian of the movement noted, "What we see in the principal biographies of the period is, in effect, only the tip of a campfire. But this is just where a study of spirituality makes its contribution to the bonfire simmering awakening!"

The Spirituality of the Great Awakening

One historian has said,

> Christian spirituality in the eighteenth century may be divided in culture, into two principal traditions. The first of these, is what we commonly associate

with monastic or hermetical life in the Middle Ages, which is the contemplative or *meditative* tradition. Early names we identify with it are St. Bernard of Clairvaux, Thomas à Kempis, and St. John of the Cross. The other tradition, vigourous in the early church and modeled in men like St. Augustine and John Wyclif, is that of the active evangelical life, what we might call *missionary* tradition.

Further, it has been said,

The age of Wesley is the second sort of spirituality and it is in fact the most dominant tradition among those prominent in the Great Awakening. But the call to action—a mission-oriented spirituality—has almost always had its origin in a profound encounter with meditative spirituality—an emphasis on the workings of the Spirit in the inner life, on the psychology of spiritual response, and on an intimate experience of the personhood of Jesus. In this the age of Wesley is no exception.[42]7

An old American evangelist once wondered aloud, "How can there be a deep revival in a shallow generation?" The men and women in this book have something to teach us about that—and it is clear that their answer involved neither condescension to shallowness nor imitation of it. For them, mature Christian spirituality can only grow from a mature Christian mind, and such a mind can only come to be when it has first hid itself in the mind of Christ.

---

[42] Jeffrey, David Lyle Jeffrey, ed., *A Burning and a Shining Light: English Spirituality in the Age of Wesley* (Grand Rapids, MI: William B. Eerdman, 1987).

As early as 1720, there were "Hell Fire Clubs" in London, the most famous of which was the one led by Dashwood, whose members referred to themselves as "the Monks of Medmenham Abbey." Another group at Skelton Castle was called the "Demoniacs." A sketch of the character of these clubs, and of their blasphemous and obscene publications, can be obtained from Hoxie N. Fairchild's *Religious Trends in English Poetry*.[43]

The history of English spirituality in the eighteenth century can be seen as a movement from inner to outer life, from the narrow confines of dwindling independent churches and student holy clubs boldly outward into the turbulence of society and the needy world, but also from a necessary deep inwardness of personal spirituality to the pressures of active commitment to missionary enterprise at home and abroad.

It can also be seen as a richness of interconnections that tie together faithful Christians of Anglo-Catholic, non-juror, independent dissenter, and established church communities into one seamless web of spiritual ministry to their culture. This tapestry is wider as well as more patterning, and even the specialized historian will not be able to discern. Yet from quite another point of view, some of these hidden lives of prayer may have been most central of all to the grand design—for example, Jonathan Edwards, who is remembered for his fiery sermon "Sinners in the Hands of an Angry God." Cotton Mather, who is quoted from his sermons in the early 1690s, stated, "We come hither because we would have our posterity settled under pure and full dispensation of the gospel, defended by rulers that should be ourselves."[44]

---

[43] Hoxie N. Fairchild, *Religious Trends in English Poetry* (New York: Columbia University Press, 1942), 2:28–49.

[44] Mark A. Noll, *Eerdman's Handbook to Christianity in America* (Grand Rapids, MI: Eerdmans, 1983), 115.

"LIGHT THE FIRE AGAIN!" TWENTY-FIRST-CENTURY DARKNESS

The American colonies in the early eighteenth century were well acquainted with biblical faith, knowledge, and understanding. But this is far different from the twenty-first century. which is alarmingly behind the eighteenth century's grasp of faith, and it amounts to a serious, significant difference.

The Great Awakening Revival was spiritually advanced by a great cadre of twenty-four seven evangelists who knew that there was nothing too difficult for God in Christ to do (Jeremiah 32:17, 27 NASB). It is a tremendous venture when the Holy Spirit intercedes with the messages rooted in the Bible's truth! The Holy Spirit is working on the souls of humanity, confirming convictions that reach out for human professions and everlasting repentance from God's words and not human pressure. The eighteenth century lit the revival fire that is in the sacred depository with supernatural resources of fire for Jesus Christ's church today. There is no question that there are smoldering embers anxiously awaiting to experience the stoked-up fire for the twenty-first century.

But what is the darkness in the twenty-first century? Beginning with Adam and Eve in the Bible, space cannot accommodate or categorize all the vehicles of darkness, but open your Bible or secure a Bible to read these verses in the New Testament: Romans 1:16–32 (NASB), Galatians 5:19–26 (NASB), and 2 Peter 2:2–22 (NASB).

The darkness has never been dormant but rather it is proactive, gathering evil to a "deep state" level in the twenty-first century from where godless darkness thrives—agnostic, atheistic, and secular humanist leaders specializing in wars; diseases (COVID-19), pestilences, disasters, hurricanes, killer hornets, homosexual deviance, volcanos, tsunamis, floods, famines, abortions, adultery, national calamities, violence, sudden deaths, renegade dictators of Hitler-like aspirations, and great ungodly powers. These things are blocking what God has intentionally provided: the all-powerful covering of the earth with the power of the Holy Spirit! But God has not abandoned us! What God has done is deposit a revival fire for us to draw from now! Today, if you hear his voice, do not turn a blind eye, a deaf ear, or a cold heart to answer God, who is calling!

The twenty-first century is making idols ("gods") of their vile passions, and these passions are loudly not God-centered. However, the real problem of the twenty-first century is not their shameful acts. The problem is that America and world Christians have quenched the faith of their forefathers in defiance of Jesus, the Christ, the Son of the Most High God. They fearlessly curse, speak blasphemously, and take Jesus's name in vain. The "People of the Lie" have become a shibboleth who are at odds with the "People of the Light!"

> For you were sometimes in darkness, but now you're
> in the LIGHT: walk as children of the light … and
> have no fellowship with the unfruitful works of
> darkness, but rather reprove them … for it is shame
> even to speak of those things which are done of
> them in secret. (Ephesians 5:8, 11–12 NASB)

Finally, if the problem is not the "darkness," the problem is the light. This dim light is like a flickering candlelight of once dedicated and courageous people who individually and corporately failed to stoke up and light the fire again. Make no mistake that the fires of the eighteenth century are ready and waiting for the twenty-first century to rekindle the embers into the fires of Jesus. There are followers who can and will stoke the embers of the fire in this century!

The fire of the eighteenth century is like a bonfire from the Bible's New Testament believers. This amazing fire is found in the Gospel of Luke. The precedent was forever set by the first-century faithful believers who attracted the "tongues like Fire burning above their heads," and they, jointly with the first century and the eighteenth century, are an incredible firsthand account to "Light." They can once more light the fires in the twenty-first century!

> And there appeared to them cloven tongues like as
> of fire, and it set on each of them; and, they were
> all filled with the Holy Spirit. (Acts 2:3–4a NASB)

> And they said to one another, "Did not our hearts
> burn within us while JESUS talked with us by the
> way; and, while HE opened to us the Scriptures?"
> (Luke 24:31–32 NASB)

THEMATIC ANALYSIS OF WILLIAM ROBINSON'S LETTER

Though dead, yet speaketh. (Hebrews 11:4 KJB)
A true Israelite indeed in whom there is no guile.
(John 1:47 KJB)

I. Cousin's letter from England dated April 10, 1740, received by Trenton, Pennsylvania, postmaster six months later, October 10, 1740. Delivered to William Robinson upon his return from months of preaching (i.e., September 1740–June 1741). William Robinson responds June 16, 1741, to his cousin in England.

Personal Joy over His Female Cousin's New Birth

II. Cousin's letter seems to have confirmed William's often hoped-for objective for some years that the natural bond of being a blood relative has given way to a dearer affection in his heart toward her. This can only mean that the two of them have been made nearer and dearer by God's grace than by nature. She's been born again, converted by grace through the help of his intercessory prayers.

III. But by the same rich and sovereign grace, God has been amplified by encircling them together in a holy embrace that will last for all eternity.

IV. William's confident trust is that she and he are both members of the same body and united to the head, which is the Glorious Christ. Further, they are together as they partake of Jesus, the bread of life, and the bread is nourished from the same fountain of the blood of Jesus's new covenant together.

V. They have different mothers, but now they have the same one Father, in one family of God. They will now, together, sit in heavenly places in Christ Jesus forever.

VI. There was great relief and great gratitude of this blessed missive to lift his soul and spirit in positive movement of refreshing encouragement of the power of the Holy Spirit. Just writing these wonderful heavenly treasures that they now share together is rapturous, and he wishes it were only possible to embrace her as a fellow sojourner for Christ here and hereafter.

VIII. Though God's purposes have taken him a distance from his father's house and relations, besides a similar distance between she and he, he cannot be depressed. No, William blesses God for all the bounties of Providence in this heavenly supply that more than compensates for the blessings of his earthly relations.

VIII. However, this is not to say how joyfully happy he would be to see her face-to-face! Though the prospects of this do not at this point seem likely, we shall ultimately see each other. This meeting may be to meet at our Lord's throne in the kingdom of glory above. There, we will no longer be separated.

IX. And now, while we are pilgrims on this earthly way, let us look unto our glorious Forerunner. For now, we must live by faith as I have always done. As other sojourners in their peregrination (transversing; walk or travel over) through this strange land below, let our focus be immovably fixed on earth, upon our amiable and immaculate righteousness wrought by our incarnate God by both the active and passive obedience we give to his word.

The Focus upon Firepower and God and Heaven in William Robinson's Ministry

X. Oh, what a splendid and unfading raiment God provides for us here. Oh, let us always meditate upon this raiment and rest assure that surely the fire of love will not only kindle, burn, and burst forth in a glorious bonfire consuming all the dross in our human failings while refining us into pure silver for God's glorious raiment.

XI. Beyond our splendid Godly raiment, as we look upward and behold our blessed Emmanuel enthroned in the majesty of heaven's greatest glory and dignity, managing the reins of government for all his unfathomable creation.

XII. We can see God is altogether lovely in his transcendent beauties and yet uncreated and unfolded creations. Oh, how his radiant charms and inimitable excellence dwell upon his countenance.

XIII. Upon this earth there is not, and up in the heavens there is not. Neither humans nor angels can begin to touch our God's countenance or the infinity of his plentitude.

XIV. Words are woefully inadequate to describe what an immense and unfathomable ocean of grace, mercy, and love is in his presence.

XV. Behold his unutterable sufficiency and the infinite wisdom, unsearchable power, compassion, and goodness of this blessed King, our Mediator!

XVI. Oh, let him dwell on our souls day and night as a pomander (box; hollow fruit-shaped ball) of myrrh between our breasts.

XVII. Oh, let us ever be ravaged with his beauty and satisfied and transported with his love.

XVIII. Do we experience lack of self-worth and weakness of our flesh to complement our higher spiritual longings, and does ignorance of how great our God is in all of our weakness accuse and invade us? Note the many fiery darts of Satan, which by policy and power are constantly arrayed against our shaky past and intimidated present.

XIX. But hark, the voice of truth I hear! Here in our Great Shepherd is our Great Refuge and Great Commander with all wisdom and strength to totally and safely guide us through the seen and unseen roadblocks, always protecting us and defeating our shrinking from Jesus Christ's enemy.

XX. Do swelling and insuperable mountains of temptations, discouragements, and guilt arise before us? Lo, here's an ocean of grace, mercy, and love to sink, overwhelm, and bury the loftiest insuperable mountain!

XXI. Heads of all temptations, discouragement, guilt, and darkness spread over us. Here is the inextinguishable fountain of light! Are we threatened by the stirring and boiling storms over us on the darkest night?

XXII. Look! There is a silver lining of calmness breaking through the gathered darkness, and there is a bonus! Behold a fountain of cleansing blood to wash in and remove the barnacles of temptations, discouragements, guilt, and blemishes.

XXIII. We must always remember when we turn one eye upon ourselves and our guilt, blemishes, vileness, and loathsomeness, we must let the other eye be fixed upon Jesus the Christ!

XXIV. We must always default to faith, whether it be but a faint glimmer or a colossal bonfire. Faint or colossal, it always works the same (e.g., mustard seed to a mountain). It is always faith stirring and boiling and working.

XXV. The result of faith's stirring, boiling, and working is a wonderful fragrance like spikenard to the nostrils of our Lord Jesus the Christ! Plus, it will prime the pump to draw forth our graces at the perfect (proper) time, and at the perfect place.

XXVI. Of no small importance, in addition to a wonderful fragrance to our Lord Jesus the Christ is the greatest soul benefit that redounds from faith's stirring, boiling, and working in our souls. Behold the soul's joy and comfort preserving by these gracious benefits are the very influences that emanate by the Holy Spirit that incarnates us.

XXVIII. The Holy Spirit's incarnation in our souls produces a holy contentment with earthly enjoyments that ennoble and greaten our minds by transforming us into the divine image of Jesus the Christ.

XXVIII. Triumph over the enemies of our soul by the stirring, boiling, and working of our faith comes laden with incalculable treasures of heavenly proportions. This precious gain of the merchandise of eternal treasure of grace (God's Riches At Christ's Expense) is forever secured in the haven of our Lord Jesus the Christ's endless glory.

XXIX. The key to faith's treasures must not be in certain acts of faith but in the living day in and day out of faith. This is possible by looking and learning upon our beloved Lord Jesus the Christ until we are totally one with him, one in him! Thus, we are encompassed and permeated with the boundless and eternal love of God in Jesus the Christ and <u>our</u> Lord and Savior!

The Focus upon Earthly Relations

XXX. But, alas, which eye shall I succeed in turning to with my earthly relations? Oh, that my poor sister might be visited with the salvation of God in Jesus the Christ. Not just my sister but my whole family in England might be regenerated and grafted by faith in Jesus the Christ.

XXXI. My greatest prayer for my family, but particularly my sister, is that infinite love may take pity upon them so they lie in the blood and not be dependent upon earthly relations or successful attainments. But that God in our Lord Jesus the Christ would drop down his love into their hearts for him and thereby infuse spiritual life into them.

XXXII. I am gladdened to hear in your letter of your brother Garthorn's family and the religious family that you have married into, though I am not of your opinion in the denomination you have chosen.

XXXIII. Just so you know, circumstantial differences (i.e., your religion choice) bear no weight upon our relationship whatsoever with me.

XXXIV. What really counts with me, and what I earnestly desire, hope, and love unfaintedly above all things, is that all people would come to love Jesus the Christ. I unflinchingly can embrace all Jesus the Christ believers regardless of denomination, because denominational choice can create no alienation of affection in me!

XXXV. I bless the name of Almighty God that he has given me a Catholic spirit toward all believers in Jesus the Christ. I am thankful that the spirit that God has given me is not a tied up spirit to some denomination or restricted to Presbyterians or, for that matter, any other denomination.

XXXVI. Jesus the Christ has set me free from the bias of denominations, so I am free to cultivate a relationship with your brother by correspondence.

George Whitfield

XXXVII. George Whitfield has informed us (Log College students, graduates, and leaders) of the work of the Holy Spirit in England. By the sound of Mr. Whitfield's report, the Holy Spirit will grow and spread revival there.

XXXVIII. The extent of the revival, I pray to God, may reach Cumberland too and beyond, as I have intimated in some of the previous parts of this letter. The increase of Christ's kingdom in the land America has not failed. Here, there have been such surprising effusions of God's Spirit in the ministry, especially under Mr. Whitfield.

Our New Brunswick Presbytery; the "Famous Tennents"

XXXIX. In addition to the surprising results under Mr. Whitfield is our New Brunswick Presbytery, in which the famous Tennents, my dear brethren, are also having surprising results.

XL. That result has affected all New England, the provinces of York, the Jersies, Pennsylvania, and Maryland, which are filled with convinced and converted souls.

XLI. Many are the thousands brought to Jesus the Christ! And on this way are children, youth, and aged persons, rich and poor, black and white. It is no great occurrence in America to preach to five thousand people, and to preach three to five times a day.

XLII. My health is not so good, yet I've preached ten times a week. Some other of our Presbytery preach twenty times a week.

XLIII. The power for this preaching proceeds from the very Spirit of God, and it is wonderful!

1. Hundreds cry out in congregations under a deep sense of their miserable lost and Christless estate.
2. Whole assemblies are turned into Bochims (i.e., "Weepers"; a village in Western Germany of the Ruhr Valley).
3. Floods of tears appear over congregations.
4. Hundreds again are melted with the love of Jesus the Christ and fade away and die almost in pangs of divine love.

XLIV. I cannot but think with all this intensity of the earthquake in thousands of lives here in America that it equals or surpasses the apostles' days. In those days, wherever the Holy Spirit came, people were filled with a zeal for God.

XLV. I would be remiss if I did not report that the enemy has controlled others with bitter rage as God's word is sent among them—again, just like the apostles' days!

XLVI. In fact, here in America, there is nothing lacking for an eighteenth-century blood-stained Persecution like in the first century, except for one thing. In America, there are barriers and boundaries that liberty provides for the free expression of faith without the death penalty! Should these liberty barriers be removed an awful scene would directly ensue.

XLVII. However, it needs to be greatly noted that the more the work is opposed, the more it grows, spreads, and indeed the Holy Spirit is adding daily to the results mentioned above.

XLVIII. Unbelievably, it is now more than a year since I was licensed ["now" is June 16, 1741] to preach and admitted to the Presbytery. In this short time, what I've written you does not begin to tell you all the great things God has done for me! And what honor God has conferred on me, a poor, ignorant wretch! Oh, that I may be humble and thankful.

XLIX. Time and space are not enough in this letter to gratify your desires to know of the many avocations of my experiences up unto this point.

Personal Items

L. Please relate my gratitude to Robert Stoddard for his kind letter and kind offices. I have never had any resentment against him. I truly desire his happiness.

LI. I beg Robert and you, and for that matter any other person who has an acquaintance with the true and vital piety, that you exert yourselves in essaying the advancement of Jesus the Christ's honor for the good of all human souls!

General Items

LII. One caveat: I pray you do not allow difference of opinions about some things hinder mutual endeavors. This commitment, dear cousin, may Brother Labor use to promote meetings of prayer and religious conferences among you. Also, my old friend Robert would do the same about him as I've asked you to do.

LIII. Now, if God has given you knowledge and grace above others, be sure to use them for the glory of the Giver thereof. I know that the Lord blessed my attempts for the conversion of many this way above I've requested of you and my old friend Robert.

LIV. Before I became a minister, I was apt to think that one's labor for Jesus the Christ will not be fruitless neither in the same laudable method (see LIII, "as having been given knowledge and grace above others.") Certainly the Lord has blessed the feeble endeavors of many in this land of America too, for much good to their friends and neighbors. Nay, much of the work is thus carried on as well as begun.

LV. Oh, try, try for the Lord Jesus's sake!

LVI. Send my very dear love to my sister and brother! Warn them of their danger and the necessity of a new heart; and the real knowledge of the saving faith in Christ Jesus.

LVII. I want directions to write to her; my love to all friends.

LVIII. I go over sundry provinces as an itinerant as I am expected to do from the order of my Presbytery. The best way to contact me, therefore, will be to direct your mail for me to the care of Mr. Thomas Noble in New York. He is a merchant who's a noted gentleman and an Israelite indeed!

LIX. If you direct your mail for me to Mr. Noble, it will come this way most safely and speedily wherever I may be.

LX. I am yours, dear cousin.—C. Wm. Robinson.

Education Institutions

LXI. P.S., The colleges of New England are now replenished with young men of quite a different stamina (thine mine).

LXII. About a year ago, there were not above eight persons in both, but what has been convicted or converted chiefly by Brother Whitfield and Mr. Gilbert Tennent's preaching.

LXIII. The salt being thus part into the fountain the streams are like to be sweet and promises yet greater things in this land of America. I cannot but think that the thousand years are beginning for Christ's reining by the Gospel over the nations. Although before in the universal, the witnesses are to be slain, and a short time of persecution will be felt by the faithful.

Converts: Quakers

LXIV. There are now many Quakers [the only denomination that believed slavery was sin] who are truly converted and baptized, and they have received the sacrament of the Lord's Supper. Many are persecuted by their parents and cast out of their houses and families, but all severities avail nothing!

LXV. Excuse my brevity and confusion, and let me hear from you, and beg my sister to write and let me know about her soul affairs. Let P. Robert write. You write and spare not—pray for us.

LXVI. I've writ as fast as possible,

THE "NEW LIGHT" PREACHING STYLE OF GEORGE WHITFIELD

October 17, 1740, he (Whitfield) had his long-awaited meeting with Jonathan Edwards. For all their shared importance to the Eighteenth Century (and perhaps because of it), the two had little in common. Edward's interests were philosophic theology and the mind, whereas Whitfield's were preaching and the passions ... and so the two came together around the cause of revival ...

Still, Edwards was an international figure in the emerging Colonist network and Northampton was on the tip of every revivalist's tongue. The meeting carried significance for both Edwards and Whitfield, and each spoke warmly of it. Whitfield later confessed, "I have not seen like [Edwards] a fellow in all New England." In all, Whitfield preached four sermons from Edwards' pulpit. The text for the opening sermon does not survive, but the theme dealt with 'the consolations and privileges of saints, and the plentiful effusion of the Spirit upon believers.' Throughout, he reminded his hearers of their long association with revivals and Northampton's pivotal place in the emerging Calvinist evangelical order. Both speaker and listeners frequently "wept much."

The following after he again preached with great success and confessed,

> "I began with fear and trembling, but God assisted me. Few eyes were dry in the assembly. I had an affecting prospect of the glories of the upper world, and was enabled to speak with some degree of pathos. It seemed as if a time of refreshing was come from the presence of the Lord."

> In the audience, Edwards felt "weak in body" and was visibly affected by the preaching. Such was Whitfield's power that by the third sermon he could report that "good Mr. Edwards wept during the whole time of exercise.'" Just as exciting, "the people were equally affected, and in the afternoon [sermon] the power increased yet more."[45]

It was important that Whitfield exhibit "power" in Edwards's pulpit, both for the revival of Northampton and for his own position in the international movement. In fact, he met with complete success. Edwards himself reported that as a result of Whitfield's preaching, "Northampton was again revived, and in about a month there was a great alteration in the town."

---

[45] Harry S. Stout, *The Divine Dramatist: George Whitfield and the Rise of Modern Evangelism* (Grand Rapids, MI: William B. Eerdmans, 1991), 125–26.

Seeing Sarah Edwards's (Jonathan's wife) assessment of George Whitfield's preaching at Northampton is interesting considering the acclaim and the attention her husband and she were receiving. Five days after Whitfield's visit, Sarah Edwards wrote her brother a remarkably insightful letter describing Whitfield and the recent events. In terms of method, she wrote, "He makes less of the doctrines than our American preachers generally do and aims more at affecting the heart. He is a born orator." The effects were spectacular:

> It is wonderful to see what a spell he casts over an audience by proclaiming the simplest truths of the Bible. I have seen upwards of a thousand people hang on his words with breathless silence, broken only by an occasional half-suppressed sob … A prejudiced person, I know, might say that this is all theatrical artifice and display; but not so will anyone think who has seen and known him.[46]

For his part, Whitfield was much taken with Sarah Edwards, whom he found "adorned with a meek and quiet spirit." He would subsequently look upon her as a model for the type of wife he hoped to find."[47]

As it was in succeeding generations, particularly the twentieth century with Billy Sunday and Billy Graham, the successful style of Whitfield itinerant's ministry was successful.

The following is the account of 1740 evangelist admirers of Whitfield and his style.

---

[46] Ibid.
[47] Ibid., 126–27.

Throughout western Massachusetts and the Connecticut River Valley, Whitfield kept up his grueling pace of twice-daily preaching, discoursing often on grace, election, and the dangers of an unconverted ministry. Along the way he encountered clerical admirers and would-be imitators such as Eleazar Wheelock, Benjamin Pomeroy, Andrew Croswell, and James Davenport (whom he had met in Philadelphia, and who shared his suspicions about unconverted elders). All of these young men found in Whitfield's stirring denunciations the rhetoric they needed to challenge authority and encourage lay separations.

Inevitably, these young imitators threatened established authority and strained relations between congregations and their local pastors, and suddenly the potential for conflict in these revivals became vividly apparent. Whitfield's dramatic characterizations were one thing, but his confrontational, us-against-them rhetoric contained the seeds of trouble that even he would live to regret in the deranged ministry of one James Davenport.

For the moment, however, all remained relatively calm as churches focused their enthusiasm and zeal on Whitfield's preaching.[48]

In William Robinson's letter, he refers to his own and other associates of the Great Awakening (e.g., George Whitfield and the Tennent

---

[48] Harry S. Stout, *The Divine Dramatist*, 128–30.

Family) and their evangelism: "I cannot think but what it equals or surpasses the apostles day wherever it comes people are filled with zeal for God, and others with bitter rage as word is sent among them."

In Hartford, Connecticut, Pastor Daniel Wadsworth looked forward to Whitfield's visit with great anticipation. Already in February, Wadsworth had received a copy of Whitfield's sermons with prefatory letters by Benjamin Colman and Josiah Smith. The advance publicity had whetted his appetite and that of his congregation, who heard Whitfield at Hartford in the morning at Wethersfield in the afternoon. Whitfield's afternoon sermon was a favorite from 2 Corinthians 5:17 on regeneration, in which he enacted the birthing of a "new creature" transformed by saving grace. Wadsworth had never witnessed such a performance. The truth of the doctrine of the new birth could not be doubted, but the manner of presentation was a different story: "What to think of the man … I scarcely know." Two months later, Wadsworth was still struggling, this time over the *Journal*: "met with the famous Mr. Whitfield's life and read it. But what is it?"

If the clergy were both moved and uncertain, there were no such reservations on the part of ordinary men and women. In Middletown, Connecticut, as Whitfield addressed a moderately large crowd (for him) of four thousand, a local farmer named Nathan Cole described the event in his private diary.

His words would be discovered years after his death and widely reprinted in the twentieth century. Scholars find in his account a perfect description of the popular enthusiasm and frenzy that accompanied a Whitfield sermon.

Reports from Philadelphia that Whitfield preached "like one of the apostles" had raised Cole's interest, and he eagerly followed the course of Whitfield's itinerancy, "hoping soon to see him." Word of Whitfield's preaching in Hartford and Wethersfield raised hopes that he would also appear in Middletown. Sure enough, on the morning of October 23, a "messenger" raced through Middletown with news that Whitfield would preach out-of-doors that morning at ten o'clock. Cole's response was frantic:

> I was in my field at work. I dropped my tool ... and ran home to my wife, telling her to make ready quickly to go on and hear Mr. Whitfield preach at Middletown, then ran to my horse with all my might, fearing that I should be too late. Having my horse, I with my wife soon mounted ... We improved every moment to get along as if we were fleeing for our lives, all the while fearing we should be too late to hear the sermon, for we had twelve miles to ride.[49]

After a furious ride, the Coles made it to the Connecticut River by Middletown. Cole struggled later to describe the novel scene before him.

> I saw before me a cloud of fog arising. I first thought it came from the great river, but as I came nearer the road I heard a noise of horses' feet coming down the road, and this cloud was a cloud of dust made by the horses' feet. When I came within about 20 rods of

---

[49] Private diary of the 1940 sermons of George Whitfield regarding Middletown, Connecticut, farmer named Nathan Cole.

the road, I could see men and horses slipping along in the cloud like shadows, and as I drew nearer it seemed like a steady stream of horses and their riders, scarcely a horse more than his length behind another, all of a lather and foam with sweat, their breath rolling out of their nostrils every jump. Every horse seemed to go with all his might for the saving of souls. It made me tremble to see the sight.

Once Cole had stationed himself and his wife in the crowd, he turned back to the river where he saw "the ferry boats running swift backward and forward bringing overloads of people, and the oars rowed nimble and quick. Everything, men, horses, and boats seemed to be struggling for life."

The sermon that followed did not disappoint an expectant Cole. When Whitfield climbed the scaffolding assembled for his visit, "he looked almost angelical: a young, slim, slender youth, before some thousands of people with a bold undaunted countenance." Soon Cole was caught up in the moment by a master of gesture and presence who "looked as if he was clothed with authority from the Great God." So powerful was the sermon, Cole concluded, that it "gave me a heart wound ... I saw that my righteousness would not save me."[50]6

It is easy to see why Cole's description is so widely reprinted. It captures, as no ministerial diary could do, the popular impact that Whitfield exerted on ordinary listeners. There was no pretext of analysis or critical description but rather a language that strained to reproduce a novel experience in powerful, image-filled words. The

---

[50] Ibid.

references to shadowy figures, thunderous noise, and clouds of dust point, as no official account could, to the powerful emotions evoked by Whitfield's preaching.

In two short months, Whitfield had become the darling of New England. Such was the inherited piety of ordinary New Englanders that his preaching was like "putting fire to tinder." Their long tradition of local revivals fed into a mass event of nearly universal proportions. And for once, Whitfield learned as much as he gave. Never before had he seen such uniformly high levels of popular piety and Calvinist knowledge. Family worship, he observed, "is generally kept up," and "the blacks are better used than in any province I have yet seen. On many accounts," he concluded, New England "certainly excels all of provinces in America; and, for the establishment of religion, perhaps all other parts of the world."[51]

---

[51] Ibid.

POSTLUDE

Isaac Watts: "The Saints Unknown in This World"

Out of the millions of mankind that spread over the earth in every age ... GOD has been pleased to take some of HIS own family, has given them a heavenly nature, and made them HIS sons and daughters.

But HE has set no outward mark of glory upon them – there is nothing in their figure or in their countenance to distinguish them from the rabble of mankind. AND, it is fit that they should be in some measure, unknown among their fellow mortals ...

The life of the Saints is hidden with Christ in God. But when Christ, who is their life, shall appear with HIM in glory ... in that day they shall stand forth before the whole creation in fair evidence; they shall shine in distinguished light, and appear vested in their own undoubted honors ...

Somewhere, we may suppose, sometime before all these remarkable events of revival began, there was one or dozens, or hundreds, but perhaps just one person praying.[52]

Thus will it evermore be with William Robinson and other multitudes for whom there is not a lot of existing biography information.

---

[52] Public domain.

EPILOGUE

Rev. Samuel Davies has celebrated the labors and successes of William Robinson's service to God in one of his poems; Rev. Davies was also an eighteenth-century hymn composer.[53] Mr. Gilbert Tennent speaks of Robinson as "that wonderful man." Davies was one of the earliest missionaries to slaves in the English colonies. He was also the pastor of Patrick Henry, whose oratory skills were honed by Davies.[54]

The power behind Patrick Henry's famous speaking ability lay in his popular, homespun style that was often peppered with biblical references. Henry, an Anglican, successfully used the evangelical rhetorical mode in revolutionary politics. As a teenager, Henry had often listened to Samuel Davies and sermons by other Virginia Presbyterians. Henry's uncle and namesake, the Anglican priest Patrick Henry, feuded incessantly with Presbyterians in Hanover County. On Patrick Henry the nephew, however, the Presbyterian's style made a more favorable impression. Henry reportedly called Davies "the greatest orator he ever heard." Some acquaintances reckoned that Henry spoke like an evangelical minister and that "his figures of speech … were often borrowed from the Scriptures."

---

[53] Samuel Davies, "Great God of Wonders," in *Praise! Our Songs and Hymns* (Brentwood-Benson, 1976), 294.

[54] Samuel Davies, *Letters from the Rev. Samuel Davies.*

A close examination of Henry's 1775 "Liberty or Death" speech has shown that it is full of biblical phrases, particularly from the prophet Jeremiah.[55]3

Here is William Robinson's personal testimony in his letter: "I cannot tell what great things God has done for ME, what honors conferred on me a poor ignorant wretch. Oh that I may be humble and thankful."

Though little is known about William Robinson, he made a mark on history that few can make. Robinson was a key player in the Great Awakening along with George Whitfield, the apostle of the Great Awakening.

Well done good and faithful servant. (Matthew 25:21–23 NASB)

---

[55] Public Domain.

BIBLIOGRAPHY

Alexander, Archibald. *The Log College: Biographical Sketches of William Tennent and Principal Alumni of the Log College, Together with an Account of the Revivals of Religion under their Ministry in the 18th Century.* Birmingham, AL: Solid Ground Christian, 1846.

Davies, Samuel. "Great God of Wonders." In *Praise! Our Songs and Hymns.* Brentwood-Benson, 1976, 294.

Davies, Samuel. *Letters from the Rev. Samuel Davies on Virginia Christian Slaves.* London, 1757.

Edwards, Jonathan. *Select Works of Jonathan Edwards; Sermons.* Vol. 3 Banner of Truth Trust, 1959.

Hansen, Collin, and John A. Woodbridge. *A God-Sized Vision: Revival Stories That Stretch and Stir.* Zondervan, 2010.

Hatch, Nathan O., George M. Marsden, Mark A. Noll, David F. Wells, and John D. Woodbridge, eds. *Eerdmans' Handbook to Christianity in America.* Grand Rapids, MI: William B. Eerdmans, 1983.

Jeffrey, David Lyle, ed. *A Burning and a Shining Light: English Spirituality in the Age of Wesley.* Grand Rapids, MI: William B. Eerdmans, 1987.

Kidd, Thomas S. *The Great Awakening: A Brief History with Documents.* Boston: Bedford/St. Martin's, 2008.

Kidd, Thomas S. *The Great Awakening: The Roots of Evangelical Christianity in Colonial America.* New Haven, CT: Yale University Press, 2007.

Knight, Walter B. *Knight's Master Book of New Illustrations.* Grand Rapids, MI: W. B. Eerdmans, 1965.

Lambert, Frank. *Inventing the "Great Awakening.* Princeton, NJ: Princeton University Press, 1999.

McCullough, David. *John Adams.* Simon & Shuster, 2001.

Morris, Benjamin Franklin. *Christian Life and Character of the Civil Institutions of the United States: Developed in the Official and Historical Annals of the Republic.* Nabu Public Domain Reprints.

Noll, Mark A. *Eerdmans' Handbook to Christianity in America.* Grand Rapids, MI: Eerdmans, 1983.

Robinson, William. Personal letter, June, 1741.

Ryrie, Charles Caldwell. *Ryrie Study Bible: New International Version.* Expanded ed. Chicago: Moody, 2008.

Scougal, Henry. *The Life of God in the Soul of Man.* Fearn: Christian Focus, 1996.

Sprague, William B. *Annals of the American Pulpit; or Commemorative Notices of Distinguished American Clergymen of Various Denominations: From the Early Settlement of the Country to the Close of the Year Eighteen Hundred and Fifty-five.* Vol. 3. New York: Carter, 1858.

Stout, Harry S. *The Divine Dramatist: George Whitefield and the Rise of Modern Evangelism.* Grand Rapids, MI: William B. Eerdmans, 1991.

Introduction to Athanasius. Crestwood, NY: St. Vladimir Seminary, 1993.

Various Denominations: From the Early Settlement of the Country to Close of the Year 1855. Vol. 3. New York: Carter, 1858.

Webb, James H. *Born Fighting: How the Scots-Irish Shaped America.* New York: Broadway, 2004.

Whitfield, George. *A Continuation of the Reverend Mr. Whitfield's Journal from His Arrival at Savannah to His Return to London.* London: James Hutton, 1739.

Whitfield, George. *Personal Journal.*

Whitfield, George. *Private Diary of the Sermons of George Whitfield.*

Wright, Esmond. *Causes and Consequences of the American Revolution.* Chicago: Quadrangle, 1966.

http://en.wikipedia.org/wiki/Carlisle_Cumbria

http://www.history1700s.com/articles/article1066.shtml

http://mason.gmu.edu/~alaemmer/disease/smallpox.pdf, p. 4

http://listverse.com/2009/06/20/10-illnesses-and-their-effects-on-history/
The Sixth Most Well Known Disease, p. 3

http:/www.puritansermons.com/banner/sdavies1.htm

Printed in the United States
by Baker & Taylor Publisher Services